300 Horror Writing Prompts

BY: JULIE WENZEL

300 Horror Writing Prompts

ISBN: 9781726888394

To contact the author visit:
www.jmwenzel.com

Author: Julie Wenzel
Cover Art by: Julie Wenzel

TABLE OF CONTENTS

FOREWORD

There are so many ways to tap into a reader's fears and emotions through horror. However, scaring a reader is more than just picking a theme or phobia and running with it. In order to truly frighten a reader, one must consider why someone may be afraid of something to begin with. From there, expand the reader's imagination of all the *what-ifs* in hypothetical dark scenarios. Put yourself in their shoes.

For this prompt book, I worked on creating a mixture of ideas from serial killers, zombies, forgotten asylums, and psychological torment. However, prompts only can take a story so far. It is up to you as the writer to take it to that next level. These are just starters to spark your imagination.

There is such a wide spectrum of horror. It is up to you on how far you take it. Will you focus on the lead character's mental conflicts? Will your story be purely a slasher horror? What do the characters have to lose? What is the motive of the tormentor?

The direction you take these horror prompts is entirely up to you. Don't feel restricted in the direction you take your horror stories. Make your stories as frightening or parody as you wish.

Enjoy the writing process! Write the story you want to tell.

JULIE WENZEL

HOW TO USE THIS BOOK

You are 100% free to use these story starters for your own personal projects such as a novel or script you are selling commercially. You cannot use these prompts in a *stand-alone* manner. Meaning, you cannot use these prompts word for word for a prompt book of your own. These prompts are meant to inspire you to create something of your very own such as a short story, novel, movie, or video game script.

In this book, you will find a mixture of prompts such as slasher horror, paranormal, thriller, mystery, psychological, zombie apocalypse, and more.

Some prompts are written with questions at the end. Some are written more like a book blurb or excerpt from a novel. Some prompts are lengthy. Others are as short as a sentence or two. Everyone is inspired differently. Therefore, the prompt styles in this book will vary.

One thing to keep in mind with a horror prompt book is you are in control of the scare level in your stories. If a prompt is too frightening for your taste, tone it down. If a prompt is too mild, crank up the terror. As an extra challenge, consider turning some of your stories into a comedy horror story or parody.

A few ways to use books:

- Think of a random number or roll some dice.

- Have someone else choose a number for you.

- Use these as daily writing exercises.

- Make a game or a contest with these prompts. Choose a prompt for a group of writers to use as a starting point. Vote on the best story and award prizes.

- Start at prompt number one and work all the way to 300. Force yourself to write each and every prompt.

- Write short flash fiction inspired by a prompt.

- Combine several prompts into a single epic novel.

- Use these prompts to backstories for characters in your already existing novel, script, or video game.

Artists can use these prompts to inspire their artwork.

Video game developers can use this book to incorporate story ideas into their game.

There are no rules to this book.

Use this book to exercise your writing, come up with new ideas, or to enhance your already existing stories.

SECTION 1: PROMPTS 1 - 49

1. A woman rubs electrode gel across her belly in preparation to hear her baby's heartbeat with a home fetal monitor. Just as she places the monitor across her belly, she hears a horrifying scream through the device.

2. These house flippers are not only experts in laying bathroom tile and refinishing hardwood floors, but also extinguishing any haunted element in a house. Write about a time they have an especially hard time removing the unwanted spirits.

3. Write about a zoo filled with zombie infected animals. Who visits this zoo? How are the animals fed? What happens when one day the animals get loose?

4. Write about a spaceship that is being haunted by a spirit that was once a living being centuries ago. How did it enter the ship? Why is it angry? What kind of horrors does this spirit bring to the fleet?

5. Several prestigious scientists claim that the world is going to end by a meteor strike in the next 100 days. Hysteria spreads. The world is beginning to spiral into irreversible chaos, which causes people to desperately search for an answer to stop the world's end. A cult comes forward and convinces the public that unleashing a demon onto the world is the only hope to save the planet. What is the result of this cult completing their dark summoning ritual?

6. Bones are uncovered in a ditch next to a commercial property. Detectives and forensic investigators are brought to the site to uncover who the bones belong to and how the person died. But a paranormal entity is doing everything it can to halt the investigation.

7. Write about a second-hand store that knowingly sells haunted items to unsuspecting buyers.

8. Write about a research team that is stranded in a catastrophic blizzard. While waiting for the storm to pass, they discover that they are not alone. Ghosts haunt the area. Do they escape through the blizzard or confront the tormented spirits?

9. An inmate from death row has completed his last meal and is escorted to the electric chair. Just as the large switch to his chair is turned on, he uses a superpower within him to redirect the electricity to every guard and person watching. Everyone is dead. The inmate unbuckles himself from the chair and escapes the prison. The madman now walks among civilians. He is merely getting started.

10. Write about a witch that was the one framing all the people accused of witchcraft in the late 1600s during the Salem witch trials. What was her motive? Was she ever caught for her crimes? How did she frame people? How did she convince people to believe her?

11. This old jail was the top tourist attraction in town for the last twenty years. One day, the jail comes to life with tormented poltergeists. Dozens of tourists are trapped inside. Write about this event.

12. Write about a student that has signed up to do a dream study at a historic university. During the study, their dreams turn to nightmares. Every day after that study, they find it impossible differentiating between being awake and asleep. Can this student escape their endless nightmares?

13. Write about a portal found in a janitor's closet at a high school that not only makes staff disappear but also unleashes a series of paranormal events. Who knows the portal exists?

14. A series of disappearances have been connected to people who put their house on the market. After dozens of disappearances, a retired detective puts his house up for sale to see if he can solve the mystery. No house has been sold in town for years without the owners completely disappearing first. What happens to the detective? What does he discover?

15. While on a road trip, a woman goes into labor. Her and her husband head to the nearest town and find a hospital where she is quickly admitted. But it isn't long after the birth of her child that they discover something is wrong with the hospital. Every time the couple attempts to leave, the staff finds a way to keep them locked inside. Write about this couple trying to escape with their newborn. What is off about the hospital staff? What kind of horrors do they face?

16. Choose a piece of children's classic literature and transform it into a horror story. For an extra challenge, combine several children's stories into one terrifying story. How do all the worlds collide?

17. During a weekend getaway, a couple buys a book of poetry in the signed book section of an antique shop. Over time, the wife becomes obsessed with the words in the poetry. She is convinced that there is a special meaning behind them. Strange and eerie events in their life may prove her to be right. What does she discover?

18. Write about someone who attempts to contact a dead loved one through a spiritual medium. The spirit of the dead seems to become angrier by the minute. They begin to wonder if they have connected with an evil spirit instead. What is happening?

19. You are hired as the vice-principal of a charter school. After working there for two weeks, you discover something is off about the school. No one has shadows. No one seems to eat their lunch. Every day is the same as the one before. You decide to investigate the history of the charter school and attempt to disrupt its routine. What happens?

20. A soldier comes home from the war to his family. He quickly discovers that his house has become haunted. Why wasn't it haunted before? What caused the haunting to start once he returned home?

21. An author discovers that his computer is automatically typing one or two words ahead of him if he pauses momentarily. Out of curiosity, he allows the computer to take hold of the story. The story eventually shifts from a fictional thriller to something that hits too close to home in a terrifying way. What do the words say?

22. A presidential candidate turns into a zombie halfway through his campaign. Because he is likely to win, his political party does not want to reveal that he has turned. Write about how they keep his secret. How will they continue the campaign?

23. While shark cage diving in Australia, you are suddenly surrounded by a dozen zombies underwater. What happens next?

24. During your near-death experience, you watch flashbacks of your entire life. However, you see everything with a dark twist which includes demons, pain, and fire. After you wake up, you are faced with a choice. You can either return to that dark alternate reality to live out your life but ultimately have a happy ending or continue to live out your regular life and experience misery during your final years. Which do you choose? Write about the path taken and what happens.

25. Write about a farmer that discovers a burial mound on untilled land. Does he leave the gravesite alone or decide to plant on top of it?

26. A taxi driver in Vegas enjoys making conversation while driving people to their destination, often pointing out landmarks and places of interest. While getting to know one of his customers, he learns that they are attending some sort of conference for a cult. Curious and disturbed, the taxi driver follows his guests. What does discover? Does anyone notice his snooping?

27. You purchase your childhood home in a foreclosure auction. It has been almost 30 years since you last lived there. This time though, the energy in the house seems to have shifted. You question not only if there is recent paranormal activity haunting the house, but also if the house is where a series of murders have taken place. Write about all the pleasant memories you recall from your home. How have the hauntings changed everything?

28. The monster locks eyes with mine. Nothing I do allows me to pull away from his gaze. I am completely paralyzed, with no voice to scream with.

29. Society has moved underground to safeguard against the zombie infestation. Write about the underground society and what happens when a small group decides to resurface for the first time in decades.

30. The anti-Christ that was long prophesized has brainwashed most of the world. You notice demons gaining power over the world. Disturbing rituals happen in plain sight everywhere. Write about this new world. How out of control does it get before a group decides to fight back?

31. Zombies often repeat a word or phrase that matches their final living thoughts before they turn. Write about someone who has turned. In a series of flashback sequences, explain the significance behind their final words.

32. Here I remain, trapped inside the body of an undead corpse. My mind is still intact. I am buried under hundreds of rotting bodies waiting. My mind yearns for freedom and sunlight. Will I ever see the sun again?

33. All inmates at a correction facility become infected with the zombie virus, except for one. Write a story about the inmate doing everything he can to survive. What is his weapon of choice in his attempt to break free of the zombie jail?

34. Write about how the fashion industry takes advantage of a zombie epidemic.

35. A beauty queen has gone missing and is never found. Five years later, high schoolers travel to a private cabin to drink after homecoming. Not long into the party, they find themselves fighting for their lives. Write a slasher horror where the killer is suspected to be the missing beauty queen. Is the killer the long-lost beauty queen? Or someone imitating her?

36. Write a story about a stalker that sends disturbing packages to the people he obsesses over. What does he send them? Does he ever reveal himself? What happens to his victims?

37. Your child complains that someone grabs them from under the bed every night. You search under the bed and find nothing. Finally, your kid seems to grow out their fear of their bed and doesn't run in your room at night any longer. But then one day, you feel a hand grabbing you instead. What is happening?

38. Write about a type of zombie with the power of telekinesis. Describe the benefits of this ability against the living. How are survivors able to defeat them?

39. A quiet neighbor is wrongfully accused of a crime. The harassment towards him grows as his impending trial nears. Days before the trial, a series of horrific events occur against the townspeople. Is the neighbor causing these terrifying hauntings? Or is someone else attempting to frame him of everything?

40. This art museum is rumored to trap guests inside the paintings. College art students team up with paranormal investigators to determine if the museum is haunted. Write about the investigation. Will they discover the truth or become victims themselves?

41. It's zombie hunting season! Write about how this hunting season compares to others. What are the laws that revolve around this hunt? Can you only use certain weapons? What time of the year does zombie hunting season take place?

42. You are the captain of a pirate ship. Suddenly, hundreds of zombies swim towards your ship and surround you. What happens next?

43. This wasn't a typical rodent infestation. The rats were possessed by something far beyond this world. I could hear them chewing and swallowing sharp wood splinters. The splinters didn't bother them one bit. They craved flesh. Mine.

44. A shopkeeper is selling antique home décor on an online auction site. Unknown to the buyer, the items are cursed and bring dark spirits into the home. It takes an online forum community to put the pieces together and profile this online seller. Write about what they discover about this seller. What is the motive behind selling the cursed items?

45. Passengers of the sinking ship desperately swam to any nearby floating furniture or lifeboat in sight. Their only hope was an incoming ghost ship. Fog surrounded most of it, disguising its true appearance. The only thing that was evident was the depressing and dark aura the passengers felt as they boarded. Should they have waited in the secluded ocean for real help, risking hyperthermia? What awaited the passengers that boarded the ghost ship?

46. A plague is spreading across Europe, causing people to act out in murderous ways. The only signs of the plague growing in your system before it consumes you is a rise in blood pressure and insomnia. Write about the wild murder spree caused by this plague. Can anyone stop it?

47. A dating app sends one of its users into some sort of time loop of dating. Each date feels like déjà vu. Each date is almost identical to the one before it, except each date gets increasingly more frightening. The victim cannot tell the people he dates apart, as his mind grows more distorted each day. What is happening?

48. Write about a theater prop manager that is forced to find live zombies for an upcoming production. How does the manager capture and deliver live zombies to the theater? Does anyone get hurt due to the director's irrational idea?

49. These librarians accept haunted books into their secret collection in the basement. The new janitor to the library heads down to the basement at night to clean, discovering their secrets. But instead of becoming startled by his discovery, he becomes obsessed with his findings, getting sucked into the dark horrors within the pages.

SECTION 2: PROMPTS 50 - 99

50. A man's mistress turns into a zombie just as his wife is coming home. In a panic, he chains the mistress in his shed. Write what happens when the wife discovers her?

51. Write about a zombie apocalypse that starts at the stroke of midnight on New Year's Day. Where does it begin? Does the New Year's celebration make it harder for people to realize what's going on?

52. Six prisoners are taken from their facility to be part of an experimental program. At first, they are told it is for medical and scientific advancements. However, they are instead being injected with different frightening hallucinations to test their fear tolerance. How bad do the tests get? Is there a way for them to ever escape the experiments?

53. An alien spaceship has been taken over by zombies and crash lands on Earth. Where did the ship come from? Were the zombies once human or a different species?

54. A long-lasting war initiates a military draft. After the new set of troops arrive on the battlefield, they discover something is very off about the war they are entering. Their enemy appears to already be dead and stuck in-between the spirit world and the living. How can they combat this haunted opponent?

55. Several towns have fallen victim to a series of grave robberies where the bodies are removed. Eventually, it is discovered that every grave that has been dug up belonged to a victim of a various form of cancer. What do the graverobbers want with the bodies?

56. Programmers, historians, and scientists have created the ultimate simulation program – a simulation of hell. What's first meant to be for entertainment only is later taken over by the government for immoral purposes. What is the simulation used for? What are the psychological repercussions of experiencing the simulation? Does everyone come out alive?

57. This witch has been held captive for the last seven years. Her captors have long forgotten about her. She has survived her imprisonment by siphoning and harnessing energy around her. Unbeknownst to her captors, she eventually escapes and decides to torture them from afar using her dark magic. Write about her revenge.

58. A mad scientist wishes to successfully transfer the zombie virus between species. He spends an extensive amount of time experimenting on each animal species before moving onto the next. After 15 years of research, he succeeds. What animal becomes the first to transfer the virus across species?

59. A global infestation is ruled by a zombie hive queen. Zombie hordes work together as a hive mind. Write about the zombie hive queen. How does she influence the zombie swarms?

60. No one dares look into the eyes of this ghost, as it is said you become cursed for life. One man decides to prove everyone wrong about the ghost stories. Unfortunately, he soon discovers there are many truths behind the tales.

61. This pill was created to cure a common illness. However, after six months on the market, a new side effect takes hold. Over half of the users turn into zombies. What was this medication originally intended to cure? Was turning into a zombie ever noticed during the clinical trials or was it covered up?

62. The government decides to spread an airborne version of the zombie virus all over the world by airplane. The purpose is for population control as only the strong are meant to survive. Explain how this scenario actually ends up playing out. Does anyone realize the government started the zombie outbreak?

63. My spouse no longer wants to have anything to do with me. I indirectly turned a few people into zombies. It's not like I meant to do it. Although, I still find it quite funny. Let me tell you all about it.

64. A family moves into an old farm plot with a beautiful historic home. Everything is going great until the animals start dying one by one each morning at dawn. What is additionally troubling is the dead animal looks as if it has been dead for weeks when found, not hours. What is happening on the farm?

65. Write a horror story where the main characters are a group of comedians stuck together to overcome an obstacle. Their humor helps them cope with the terrors they face. What becomes their breaking point? When do the jokes end?

66. A high school senior tags along with his girlfriend to tour a prospective college she is interested in. As the weekend goes on, things feel a little off. It is as if she is joining a cult and not a college. Write what happens that weekend. What happens after the weekend concludes?

67. An oversized root takes over all of the neighbors' lawns in this small town. Underground water pipes are destroyed. Flat yards suddenly have dirt mounds popping up where the root is overgrowing. The neighborhood soon realizes that having any physical contact with this root is a death sentence. They ignore the overgrown root for as long as they can. That is until they begin to see human bones emerging from it. What is the source of this overgrown root?

68. A postal service worker hasn't delivered any mail to this one address in his entire career, until today. When he delivers the package, he discovers something unsettling is staring at him from the window. He hopes to ignore his chilling encounter, but mail and packages start rolling in for this resident every single day. What is happening?

69. A pamphlet shows up wedged in your door. Though the imagery is of sunrises and serene mountaintop views, the message inside is beyond disturbing. The brochure states, "The Killings Start Tomorrow."

70. Over the last month, you notice the same person is commenting on every single post you make on social media. The comments increasingly grow more troubling each day. You start to become nervous to write any more posts. You could block this person but are curious as to who they are and if they have a motive. Every time you click on their profile to learn more, you get the message, "Profile does not exist." What is happening?

71. I was a zombie for the last six years. At least that's what they tell me. An antidote was created. I received dozens of surgeries to piece my body back together. I was one of the lucky ones - or so they say.
Most of the flashbacks from my zombie days are uneventful. But a few of them I obsessively can't stop thinking about. I now spend my living days trying to cope with debilitating anxiety from all of my returning memories.

72. A series of suicides all have a common theme: each person's face was painted yellow with an expression that resembles common emoticons from cellphones. What convinced all of the suicide victims to paint their faces before killing themselves?

73. Twelve scratch-off winners are given a second chance to an even bigger lottery winning. They are asked to show up on the same day to receive their prize. But before they can claim the money, they are told that there is one rule. You have to be the sole survivor. There is no turning back.

74. You are knocked out, captured, and brought to an unknown location. When you awaken, you notice that the person in front of you is holding a Voodoo doll.
She says, "I am seeking revenge against someone. I want to make sure they feel maximum pain. I'll be testing on you first. Enjoy."

75. Where were you when the apocalypse started? I was rope climbing in gym class. I was so proud of myself for reaching the top for the first time. But when I glanced down to see my teacher's expression, I noticed everyone below me was groaning and thrashing about. The real challenge was climbing down with my life and brains intact.

76. The adult son of an elderly patient calls upon a psychologist to work through some of the problems their parent seems to be facing. The psychologist spends countless hours with the patient, trying to discover why they have become so fearful of everyone. None of their medications should be causing hallucinations, nor do they have any illnesses that should have any personality altering effects. Eventually, the psychologist begins to question if it is the in-home nurse tormenting the elderly patient with abuse, drugs, and demonic rituals. The son and psychologist make attempts to investigate, but there are constant interferences. What is happening? What is the patient experiencing?

77. An investigator is working on uncovering the mystery of a dozen unsolved murders that all appear to be connected. As he furthers his investigation, he determines that he is the murderer's next target.

78. An elementary class writes penpal letters for fun. Everyone receives at least one reply. One classmate keeps their penpal through high school but never meets them in person. As they prepare to meet for the first time their senior year, the letters become disturbing. This exchange begins a series of frightening events that no simple letter can end. Write about these letters. Do they ever meet in person?

79. Write about a group of fishermen and paranormal investigators that set out to find a rumored ghost fish. Where do the rumors come from? How does the group prepare for the search? How does this fish torment the sea?

80. Deep within the catacombs of the castle, four zombies have been chained and locked up for the last hundred years. Said to be once great warriors, they remain in the castle as a form of good luck. However, one person has other plans and frees the zombies. Write about who releases them and why. What happens to the castle?

81. As you progress further into the catacomb, you discover warning messages etched into the walls. For every floor you descend, the messages become few and far between. Eventually, they stop altogether. You are now alone with only the disturbing sounds of the catacomb. Do you escape? What horrors do you face as you descend? Who were the people that left the messages behind?

82. Write about the most enchanting place on Earth. Write about its hidden history, the dark purge, and the years of terror before becoming the utopia it is known to be today. What kind of past overshadows this utopia? What happened during the dark purge?

83. An explorer and his crew complete their voyage across the sea and docks on an island they plan to colonize. As they begin to settle and build, they realize they are far from alone. Write about the horrors of this island. Are hostile locals causing them problems or is the island haunted?

84. You wake up in a cottage with no memory of how you got there. Several weapons are arranged on the table in the kitchen. A few of them already have blood on them. All of the doors and windows are sealed shut. What type of weapons are placed before you? Why are you trapped inside?

85. Write about a group of developers that have been hired to create a zombie tracking and survival app. How is the app used? How does this development team create and test the app?

86. Someone is receiving texts from a friend that is lost and being hunted by cannibals. The friend has no idea how he got there. There is no way of tracing his phone. Write either a first-person perspective or alternating points of view of surviving this cannibal society. How is he able to keep his friend alive by only sending text messages?

87. A truck driver heads to a nearby rest stop. He returns to his truck and realizes the road he originally came from has disappeared. Taking the only road available, he ends up down a dark path with no way to turn back. Where is the road taking him? What happens to the trucker?

88. "Don't worry. This won't hurt one bit," he said.
"Do you promise I'll see him again if I just do this one thing?" she asked.
"Yes. Promise. It'll be as if you two were never apart."
As the serum streamed into her veins, she realized he was lying about the pain. She briefly questioned what other lies he had told her.
But all of her thoughts and questions suddenly disappeared when her body began to burn from the inside.

89. You move into your new house. One of the first things you notice is your next-door neighbor. His face is covered by a homemade mask made of paper mache and newspaper. Some say his face was chewed off by wild dogs. Others claim a dark curse is slowly eating away at his eyes and flesh. You decide to avoid him. That is until he comes knocking on your door, screaming for help. What is happening to him?

90. Crows begin to fly straight into windows and car windshields, almost always resulting in instant death. The ones that occasionally live become angry with fiery eyes and a thirst for blood. Environmentalists later discover there are no other birds left. Forensic ornithologists conclude crows kill all the other birds moments before diving to their own deaths. What is going on?

91. Write about a room in a house that has condensed dark energy that nearly paralyzes anyone that enters. Is it possible to cleanse this room of the dark spirits? Is the heaviness too much for anyone to bear? Who owns this house? Describe the debilitating psychological and physical effects of entering this room.

92. Write about a group of housewives in the suburbs that hide the last remaining zombies in their homes. What are the zombies used for? Does anyone know their secret?

93. Kids are forbidden to visit this house on Halloween for trick-or-treating. What kind of rumors does the neighborhood share about this house?
Write about a time a few kids don't listen to the warnings. What do they discover?

94. This diner serves some of the best food within 100 miles. It's a welcoming place where locals frequent. But there's one thing you never do: ask about the bolted door next to the bathrooms. What's behind the door?

95. Just as you are about to escape the historic bed and breakfast with your spouse from a horde of zombies, the stairs collapse below you. Is this to be your last vacation, or do you find a way to survive?

96. You wake up chained to someone you have never met. A voice calls out in the room. "You must work together to survive. Let the games begin."

97. A narcissistic mother sends her adult son to an asylum as revenge for not meeting her twisted expectations. Upon arrival, the son realizes the asylum he has been admitted to has been officially closed for thirty years. Nevertheless, a small group has secretly kept it open to the most emotionally disturbed individuals.
As time passes, he realizes its secret. No one is there to get better. The goal of the asylum is to study and experiment on the patients with any humanity they have left. Does he ever escape this place? How does he cope with his abandonment issues by his family? Write a story about his time in the secret asylum.

98. This popular drug sends its user to a dark and frightening place. People are enjoying the high of being scared and then slowly slipping back into reality. A newer version of the drug hits the market. It is more potent than the original. Some claim that there is a less than a 1% chance of never coming out of your nightmare state. Write about this drug.

99. Write about a zombie version of an insect. What happens when they are impossible to control and become overpopulated? Pesticide cannot kill or prevent these insects from multiplying.

SECTION 3: PROMPTS 100 - 149

100. Throughout the city, a hazardous gas seeps into the air. Those that inhale the gas die within two to three days. But to the victim, it feels like weeks or months in an alternate dimension of horror. Write about one person or a group of people searching for the antidote to the gas's effects. Explain how time feels to the victims in comparison to reality. What kind of visions do they experience?

101. "When I get out of here, you will all be sorry."
"That is entirely impossible. For one, you will never get out of here. Secondly, I have never been sorry about anything a day in my life."

102. I wake up in the center of a cornfield with the sun scorching my flesh. I clutch my hand, noticing my fingers curled around a bloody cleaver. How did I get here?

103. A helmet is invented to give purpose to the zombies that have taken over the planet. If worn, a zombie can be controlled by remote control. Write about different things people command zombies to do with this technology.

104. Your baby is just getting old enough to hold their head up and focus better with their eyes. You begin to notice that they occasionally look behind you and instantly shudder. The older your child gets, the more frequent and obvious this gets. A few times you even swore you felt a presence or saw a quick shadow in your peripheral vision. What is your child seeing?

105. What is initially thought to be a behavioral problem in children turns out to be an early symptom of a brain and flesh decomposing disease in young adults. What are the childhood symptoms of this adult condition? What causes it? What are the effects of this disease?

106. All of your friends are playing the latest virtual reality game. You decide to buy it as well to see what the fuss is all about. After you log in, you notice that none of your friends are online, but continue to play anyway. As time passes, you realize you are stuck in the game world and are unable to tell your hands to take the set off. You are stuck, your friends are absent, and the game is getting more disturbing by the minute.

107. While visiting your grandparents, a tornado blasts through the area. You take shelter in their old-fashioned shelter.

After the storm passes, you realize you cannot escape the way you came. Your grandparents, who are also suffering from early signs of dementia, recall a tunnel in the back and suggest that route. Together the three of you journey through the underground tunnels, discovering horrors and new truths about your family. Write about the journey.

108. A cult is gaining popularity both online and at organized gatherings at local community centers and parks. Initially, it is perceived by the public as just a joke. Eventually, it grows to alarming numbers. The cult is determined to reshape society. What does this cult stand for? What rituals become normalized over time? Write about a character's first-hand view of the events unfolding and a reflection of how society didn't stop the cult when it had a chance.

109. A single parent and three children live in the middle of nowhere. Feeding them and keeping their home heated is not their only challenge. The world has fallen around them from a zombie apocalypse. They know no one that has survived. Write their survival story and the shocking things this family must do to stay alive.

110. Write about a recently discovered zombie deterrent. What is it? Is it easy to obtain or do people have to fight over it due to its rarity?

111. Write a story about a world war where one side forces humans to turn into zombies. These zombies become super soldiers (stronger, fearless, and savage) while the other side keeps its dignity and remains human. Where do the zombie soldiers come from? Are they kidnapped? Slaves? Misled youth? Which side ultimately wins?

112. It's been 2,371 days since I last saw another person. I haven't opened my mouth to speak in 164 days. The last time I spoke was because I smashed my finger and cussed. Since then, I have said nothing.

Memories of my old life are fading. Why am here? Do other humans even exist? All I remember is that so many people died before I escaped to this place. So many.

The insects are the only thing keeping my last thread of humanity sane. At least with the insects, I know something else is still alive besides myself.

113. A research facility discovers a pregnant zombie. Somehow the unborn baby does not appear to be affected by the virus. Write a story about how the researchers keep both of them alive long enough for the woman zombie to give birth to the healthy baby. What happens after the baby is born?

114. Shapeshifting zombies present another obstacle for those attempting to survive the apocalypse. What types of things to zombies shapeshift into? How is this possible? How do people protect themselves?

115. Write about a famous monument of your choice that has been holding onto a deadly virus for decades. Where is it located? Who decides to use it? What does it do?

116. A madman has captured your family. Based on the sounds in the house, everyone is still alive but in separate rooms. Write about what happens inside the house. Can your family formulate a plan to escape?

117. Researchers visit a tribe said to be almost extinct. Only a handful of people remain. With dwindling resources and nowhere to expand, there is little chance they will be able to survive their ways much longer. The researchers want to gather as much information about them including their culture, rituals, and language before the last of them die off. But they begin to discover unsettling tales.

The people of the tribe claim they haven't had new children in over a century. They explain they would have been extinct over a hundred years ago if it wasn't for them clinging to dark magic that siphons life out of others. Since they can no longer have children through living an unnaturally long life, they cling to their immortality. Do the tribesmen go after the researchers? What else does the tribe reveal?

118. A captain is to make his final voyage on a rumored haunted ship. Though the ship has never sunk before, people avoid working on it in fear of the strange things that could happen while in the middle of the ocean. The captain is reluctant to go, but to honor his life's career agrees to the voyage. He is determined to identify the source of the haunting once and for all to give sailors peace in the future. What happens during his final voyage?

119. Write a steampunk horror story about a man that uses his mechanical arm to stop the zombie virus from spreading within him. He must always keep his mechanical arm fully functional. What kind of world does he live in? How long would it take for the virus to spread across his body if his arm was damaged?

120. This TV show has contestants choose between three cages. Professional actors dressed as zombies stand in two cages. Real zombies are inside the third cage. If you find yourself in the cage of zombies, you become part of the game show forever as a zombie yourself. What is the prize for choosing correctly? Write about this game show and the contestants.

121. He is the love of my life. I refuse to let him wander off with the rest of the infected. That is why before he turned, I locked him up in my basement. I occasionally consider joining him in his cage and turning too. But for now, I just sit outside the door and talk to him. I'm sure he would've married me…someday. Yes. I'm sure he loves me back, even as a zombie.

122. Write about laws and regulations that are specifically written to keep a zombie infestation contained. Write about the people that break these laws and the repercussions. What event caused these laws to be written?

123. A child in daycare is more reserved than the other kids and usually plays alone. As weeks and months go by, the staff starts to notice this quiet child is putting together disturbing messages on the magnet letters on the fridge. What kind of things is this child writing? Are these words coming from them or a paranormal whispering in their ear?

124. New businesses pop up during the zombie apocalypse. One business thrives on looting and reselling items that belonged to the undead. Most of their revenue comes from selling clothes to consignment shops and collecting money from wallets. Another business retrieves items for the family of people that have turned such as family jewelry, photos, or lockets of hair. Write about all the ways businesses take advantage of the zombie apocalypse. Who are the customers?

125. Write about a series of mysterious fires that plague the homes of this mid-sized suburb. The firemen of the city not only face the unsolved question of how the fires begin but also the psychological terrors they experience while fighting them. What kind of horrors do the firemen experience while trying to put out these fires? Do any quit as a result?

126. A bouquet of flowers is delivered one morning to a woman after her husband goes to work. Her initial assumption is they were sent by him. She reads the included note on the card: "These are for your husband's grave."

Who sent the flowers? What is the meaning behind the mysterious note?

127. Write about a political campaign between multiple candidates. The platform most citizens are interested in is how each candidate would handle the current zombie problem. What are the various ways each candidate wants to handle the zombies? Do any of the candidates have personal or financial interest in what happens to the zombies?

128. A student studying abroad has a malicious stalker. No one cares to help them, even the police. The student is just about to fly back home to escape when they receive an anonymous text, "Running won't save you. You will be followed, but I can help you."

Write about what happens next.

129. Write a story in the point-of-view of a character that is so consumed by guilt for a crime they committed that the reality around them begins to mesh with their darkest nightmares. They hear random voices and demons speaking to them, telling them to continue down the dark path they started on. The more they obsess over their previous crime, the worse the visions and voices become. Write their story.

130. A real estate agent brings her clients to a fixer-upper home. Upon arriving, they notice squatters have been living there. Not only are the squatters still in the home, but they are also hunched over and eating the brains of what appears to be another real estate agent. What happens next?

131. My grandpa hasn't been technically alive for the last five years. I have been cashing in his retirement checks this entire time. I don't feel bad about it though. I still have to take care of him. He's been locked up in my spare room, eating brains, and groaning about random nonsense. Brains aren't cheap.

132. A new form of punishment is introduced. Criminals are sentenced to relive their life from their earliest memory. But instead of living out their lives the way they remember it, every good memory is replaced with a depressing alternative. What does this do to their mental state once they are brought back to reality?

133. A hurricane sweeps across the coast. Piles of defeated zombie carcasses wash ashore. Who discovers them? Where did all the carcasses come from? Why was this zombie outbreak unacknowledged by the rest of the world? Is there still a threat somewhere?

134. The last survivors of the zombie apocalypse escape to Mars. Shortly after setting up the new world, a zombie emerges from one of the storage closets. It is the captain. He was perfectly fine during the voyage. How did he get infected? Do the survivors have to deal with a new wave of zombies or do they contain the virus before it spreads?

135. Write about a monster that feeds off fear to survive. However, it cannot present itself physically to anyone. Any fear it creates must be without showing itself to its victim. How does it accomplish scaring people?

136. Inseparable best friends since grade school suffer a traumatic attack late one night. Only one survives. The survivor is overcome with grief, feeling lost without her. That is until she receives a message from the other side. She is convinced her best friend is speaking to her from the grave and guiding her to the killer. Write the story of the surviving friend and how the messages are directing her to the killer to seek justice.

137. An earthquake traps people inside an underground parking ramp. At first, everything appears to be just a typical natural disaster rescue mission. But when the sun goes down, everyone except for one person transforms into bloodthirsty monsters. How did everyone change? What kind of creatures did they turn into? Write about a character's attempt to survive the underground parking ramp wreckage.

138. While most zombies groan nonsense and move as a group, this one is different. Not only does it stand separate from the group, it obsessively scratches the same phrase over and over on every surface. What is it writing? Write about its meaning.

139. An author is working on his latest novel. Every time he switches to the point-of-view of one of his lead characters, strange occurrences happen in his house. He is beginning to fear alternating points-of-view because of this. What is happening? What is causing these frightening events?

140. This dating app is designed exclusively for people who have experienced paranormal activities or consider themselves spiritual mediums. Write about people who meet each other through this app.

141. Zombie Live Cam is a government-funded program that allows people to watch wild zombies live on a 24-hour video feed. Write about Zombie Live Cam. Why was it created? Why is this program widely accepted? What do people witness on the live cam?

142. Write about a tourist camp set up too close to a vampire family's residence. The vampires crave the tourists' blood. One vampire plans to stand up against them and protect the humans. What happens to the tourists? Is the lone vampire able to protect them?

143. Society attempts to weed out people that are thought to be weak. To be given food, shelter, and a job, one must partake in a set of trials. The final stage is to team up with three others and survive a massive horde of zombies. How did society come to this point? What happens if you try to avoid the trials? How often do people survive the trials?

144. There always seems to be something off about the people treated at the mission hospital, yet no one can put their finger on what. Write about a family member that is convinced the hospital altered the person they love. They intend to investigate this hospital but are encountering countless obstacles. How has this family member been transformed? What is eventually discovered about the mission hospital?

145. A group of students visits a local carnival to play in the arcade and go on the rides. Their last stop for the night is a mirror maze. At first, it appears to be a typical mirror maze. Midway through, they notice that their reflection is aging. The farther they go, the older they get. Now they fear to complete the maze, afraid that death is at the end. What is happening to them?

146. "You would never understand the horrors I experienced while I was a zombie," he says.

"We rescued your mind from that decaying body – the least you can do is try to explain what it was like."

"There are lots of blank areas in my memory, which is probably for the best."

"Just do the best you can."

"Do we still have a deal? If I tell you my story, you will find me a new body?"

"Promise."

147. I could never stop eating brains, but sometimes I need a little variation with my recipes. So far, I have taken cooking and bartending courses to discover ways to spruce up my regular intake of brains. Determined to discover the most delicious ways to consume brains, I start a pilgrimage to study world cuisine.

148. This asylum near the edge of the city has been running since the 1800s. Everything seems normal about it, as it has a professionally designed website, online reviews, and an outdoor fenced area that residents spend time in. But it turns out to be all an act. The asylum mysteriously burns to the ground in the middle of the night and unleashes the monsters that were hiding within. Write the story of this asylum's history and the aftermath of the fire.

149. A young child is obsessed with lining her toys up in front of the TV and radio. Her parents are concerned she has autism due to her other various obsessions and the fact that she talks very little.

While being evaluated, she exhibits the same behavior. Only this time, out of nowhere, she turns to everyone and says, "I do this because they make me." Then she goes back to lining up her toys.

The parents eventually decide to call in a medium.

The medium feels a chill in the house.

"Your daughter is essentially trapped by these toys. There are spirits attached to them. They wish to be near radio and satellite frequencies and use your daughter for it."

Is this true? How do the parents react to it? What needs to be done to free the girl from her possessed toys?

SECTION 4: PROMPTS 150 - 199

150. Write about an abandoned zoo that is said to be haunted. A group of curious people sneaks into the zoo to see if the rumors are true. What they quickly discover is the animal ghosts can cross over from the spirit world and attack those in the world of the living. Who dares enter this zoo?

151. Write about zombie mermaids that sing haunting and seducing tunes similar to that of a siren's. Who falls victim to their songs?

152. This traveling business claims to have the ability to remove any paranormal activity in your home. However, their business is all run on lies. Despite having their own television show and podcast following, they have never successfully removed ghosts from a home. Write about a time they find themselves in a situation where they have no choice but to find a way to combat the spirits and remove them for good.

153. This version of the zombie virus is a slow and lengthy process to complete. Someone bitten could live for up to a month before the virus completely takes over. Write a story about a person that has days left to live before the virus completely consumes them. How do they spend their final days? What do they think about the days and hours before turning?

154. A bookworm who can read a novel in a day stumbles across a book in the library they have never heard of. As they proceed through the chapters, they find something very familiar with the novel. They question if they wrote the novel themselves but have no recollection of doing so. What does the book uncover? Does it predict the future or reveal a dark past? If they did write it, why wouldn't they remember?

155. Write a story about a farmer digging up a body that shows evidence of a zombie attack. In the months to follow, more bodies turn up. Who is trying to cover up zombie attacks by burying the victims? Is society at risk?

156. Something is wrong with Dan from IT. He's been sweating bullets for two days now. Black rings circle his eyes on his yellowing face. He flinches at every sound and is starting to slur his words. I'm keeping my eye on him. Something is off.

157. Write about someone who scans through the photos on their phone and discovers disturbing images they do not remember taking. Each photo timestamp has a different date. What are the photos of exactly? How did they get there?

158. The entire country goes black. At first, people suspect it is an enemy interfering and hacking the power grid. Eventually, top intelligence officials conclude it is hostile poltergeists. Is there any way to convince the spirits to stop tampering with the power? What made them so upset to act in such a bold manner?

159. A sinister face peers down at her every time she looks up. When she goes to sleep, it is there. When she looks up at the sky, it is there. When she uses the restroom and looks up, it is there. What is this face? How does she cope with such a horror following her everywhere?

160. Just as you believe to have survived a horde of zombies, a tornado launches dozens of them in your direction. Shrapnel from the wind has also injured you. What happens next? Is it possible to survive?

161. Pizza delivery! Right before you grab the pizza box from the delivery driver, you notice a horde of zombies standing right behind him. Describe the scene that follows.

162. I woke up in this prison. No one will tell me why I am here. They threatened to put me in solitary confinement if I ask again. Perhaps that's safer than my jail cell. My cellmate keeps saying she can only handle three more days until her thirst for blood goes out of control.

163. A forest fire wipes out hundreds of acres of a protected forest. Years later, after everything starts to grow back, it is obvious that the forest has erected an angry and haunted version of itself. Many want to burn the forest back down because of its dark aura, but protesters fight to maintain the protection of the land as it always was.
Write about the horrors the forest creates in the surrounding area. Why are so many determined to destroy it? Why are the people trying to protect it? What is their objective? Do they understand the hauntings they strive to maintain by keeping it intact?

164. This type of zombie utilizes a psychological hunting technique to lure in victims. The infected can speak coherent phrases, whimper for help, or talk about past memories. Write about a group of survivors that must endure this variety of zombie and the emotional toll it takes on them.

165. Racehorses are injected with a zombielike virus, allowing them to run at impossible speeds. After the race, an antidote is administered before they turn completely. Write about the day of a championship race when a horse is not given the antidote in time.

166. You enter a small roleplaying convention located in a rural town. Over a hundred people attend, staying in designated cabins where they can work on their costumes and plan the upcoming days.

It only takes the first day for you to realize something is very wrong with the convention. People are dressing up and acting in character, but death is real and permanent. You realize it is a new kind of cult that uses roleplaying games as a way to commit mass suicide together. You want to escape, but the other players are determined to keep you there.

167. The devil himself has come to create chaos in the world in the form of a handsome celebrity. He eventually becomes the leader of a powerful country. You are the only person that knows who he is...and he knows you know.

168. As the house burns to the ground, the firemen can hear screams coming from inside. The strange thing is, the owners swear no one is inside. What is happening? Are the screams coming from the living or the dead?

169. A couple goes to a cabin in the mountains for a romantic getaway. A blizzard traps them inside for days with over twenty inches of snow right outside their door. When the snowfall stops, they begin the grueling task of shoveling themselves out and making a path to the main road. But under the snow, they find frozen body after body. How did the bodies get there? Is the couple safe?

170. The zombie virus has spread across a romantic vacation cruise ship. Write about the fight for survival. What happens when those on land realize that the incoming cruise ship about to dock is full of flesh-eating zombies?

171. As the flood water rises, you take refuge on the roof of your house. You soon notice a horde of zombies swimming in your direction. With no weapon at hand, what do you do next?

172. Write a story from the point of view of a police officer on his first day of work when a zombie virus breaks out. What does he do to survive? Does he help others or does he only save himself?

173. People believe their savior has returned to Earth. He is everything people expect from his looks to demeanor. Over time, his followers become obsessed with everything he says and does. Each day, he does something a little more disturbing than the day before yet his followers are not phased by it. Over time, it is clear to the skeptics he is controlling people with cult-like behavior. Blood sacrifices and other horrible rituals take place in the name of this "savior." Write about a small group of people attempting to take this cult down.

174. How would zombies be fought and defeated in medieval times? Which weapons would be the most useful? Would moats be useful against zombies or would they outsmart them? Write about a time a kingdom had to defeat waves and waves of zombies. For an extra challenge, consider writing a historical horror fiction about a zombie infestation.

175. In an asylum forgotten by society, horrifying experiments take place. Victims are turned to zombies before excruciating tests are conducted. Write a first-person story about an asylum patient that begins to realize they are next in line for the experiments.

176. You find an old videotape of your 4th birthday. While watching it, you notice someone you do not recognize staring blankly in different scenes. Trying to remember who this person is, you watch the video again and notice this person is slightly transparent. Who is this person? Why are they in your birthday video?

177. A towering wall is created to protect society from the hordes of zombies. For years, the wall keeps them safe. Then one day, the zombies learn to burrow underground and travel by tunnel. Write about the next invasion when zombies pop out of the ground like weeds.

178. He is trapped inside the body of a beast yet his old mind is intact. His new body thirsts for blood with the instinct to do the unimaginable. What does his body make him do? What happened to his old body? Does he try reclaiming his previous life or surrender himself to his new body?

179. Four buddies drive cross country to witness different aspects of the zombie apocalypse. The trip eventually takes a turn for the worse. Do they make it home alive?

180. World Zombie Olympics prove to be worth the risk. Tickets sell out. Merchandise is highly sought out by collectors across the world. What kind of competitions are there?

181. Though most zombies either travel in a general horde or alone, this group maintains staying together as a family. Write about this zombie family. Consider writing flashback sequences that reflect and compare their past to their new zombie existence.

182. Write about a little girl that is convinced that her piano playing summons her imaginary friends. Where are the voices coming from? Is this a paranormal occurrence or is she suffering from a form of schizophrenia?

183. A virus has spread across the world at a rapid pace. Scientists believe to have discovered a cure and start administering the remedy as fast as they can. What they didn't expect was the cure's side effect is worse than the virus itself. What happens to those that received the new drug?

184. After a Halloween party, several people end up missing. Detectives soon discover that everyone that has gone missing was wearing a similar costume. What was the costume? Why was this significant to the kidnapper?

185. Finely diced human brains somehow end up in canned soup at the supermarket. How did they end up in the cans? Write about the secrets that are going on at the soup factory. Who discovers the brains in their bowl of soup?

186. You wake up in the middle of a cornfield, hearing whispers in the wind. Depending on the direction you take, the voices get louder or softer. As you realize the silence is more frightening than the voices, you follow the voices through the field. Where do they take you?

187. While out on a hike, a couple discovers a tree with facial features. Just as they are about to take a selfie with it, the features become more distinct and the tree screams through its mouth. The horrifying moment is captured in time with their cellphone camera. When attempting to show their friends the tree, the face is gone. What is the mystery behind this tree? Why did a face form when the couple was near it the first time?

188. A young family purchases a house that has been abandoned for years and plans to renovate it. While taking the cupboards apart, a bloody knife pops out of one of the drawers and falls onto the ground. Where did the knife come from? Is the family in immediate danger?

189. You accept a sales job with a vague description of what you are selling. Based on everything you learned about the product and company, you assume you will be selling standard medical equipment. On your first day, you realize you are selling crime scene clean-up kits for serial killers. The company has too much info on you to quit. You fear for both your life and your family's life. What do you do to break free? Write about the customers you encounter and the crimes they have committed.

190. A friend you haven't seen in twenty years messages you on social media and wants to catch up. You eagerly meet up with them. While talking to them during lunch, you notice something is off about them. It is as if they are soulless and just a talking skeleton. There is no light in their eyes. What happened to them? Is this meet up a trap?

191. Write about a young child that was trained to survive the zombie apocalypse. Who trained them? Where did their parent or guardian go? Do the horrors of the apocalypse cause any permanent psychological damage?

192. "Welcome to the other side. If you want to survive, you have to
   convert as many people as possible."

   "I don't think I'm cut out to eat brains," he says.

   "You have no choice. You either embrace this life or die. We
   can search for a cure later. But as long as we are being hunted by
   living humans, we won't be able to focus our resources on
   research."

   "Can't we just tell them the truth?"

   "No. Every time we try to speak it comes out as nonsense to
   them. Zombies don't speak coherent sentences out loud. You
   and I are currently speaking telepathically. Haven't you figured
   that out by now?"

193. Demon possessions are spreading faster than any illness in
   recorded history. Only a small group of people know how to
   conduct an exorcism. Killing the possessed is found ineffective
   because the demon will either hop bodies or keep the dead body
   animated. Therefore, the possessed are imprisoned in blessed
   buildings all over the world.

   Write about a society tormented by rampant demon possessions.
   What does society do when there is nowhere else to put
   everyone? Is there any way of saving humanity from the wave of
   demons possessing the world?

194. The spread of the zombie infestation starts during a mosh pit at a rock concert. Because of the music and excitement of the crowd, no one realizes what is happening until all hell breaks loose.

195. Write about a society that disfigures people's appearances as a form of punishment for crimes. The more crimes you commit, the more your appearance declines. Serious crimes result in a more damaging appearance. This is a way to humiliate and further punish criminals. People quickly become outcasts based on appearance.

What happens to people born with disfigurements? Are people with money able to go through reconstructive surgery and fix their appearance or is this practice illegal?

196. Write a modern-day *Frankenstein* type story where scientists try to create life. They attempt to piece together elements from an assortment of animals and humans to give their creation advanced abilities. What are the repercussions of their creation?

197. After the successful extermination of the zombies, religious cults arise in honor of the undead. Write about these cults and their beliefs and rituals. Do they ever attempt to reintroduce zombies back into society?

198. When a witch's husband becomes terminally ill, she becomes obsessed with forbidden spells of transferring someone's soul into another body. In preparation of the soul transfer, she practices on small animals and eventually other humans. Write a story about her horrifying witchcraft that slowly haunts the people that live around her. What are the repercussions of her experiments? Does she ever attempt to move her husband's soul into another body or does he die before then?

199. You return home after a long night of drinking and wake up with fresh puncture wounds on your neck. At first, you figure it is just a spider bite but realize something is also wrong with your body and mind. At noon you receive a text message that reads: "Last night I bit you. You were too easy. If you want to live, I need you to kill someone for me. Respond to this message to find out more. You won't survive the vampire transformation. Trust me. You are nothing but a weak, drunken fool."

SECTION 5: PROMPTS 200 - 249

200. You visit a popular restaurant with rave reviews on a busy Saturday night. After receiving your meal, you notice worms in your salmon dinner. You complain, but the restaurant staff doesn't believe you. Even the person you are with thinks you are lying as they cannot see the worms you are showing them. You suddenly notice worms in your friend's food as well. Being the only person who can see the worms, you become hysterical. You jump up from your seat and look at the plates of food other people are eating from. You notice worms in every single dish but are the only one that can see them. What is going on?

201. Write about a cooking competition that throws the contestants into an arena against each other filled with psychological and physical torture. Are any of the contestants there willingly? What is the prize for winning? What happens to those that lose? Explain what kind of obstacles they have to overcome to finish their dishes for the judges.

202. You flip through your phone and discover a photo of yourself. At first, it looks as if you are sleeping. After enhancing the brightness, you notice your eyes are open and you look lifeless. How does this photo exist?

203. A special task force is established to prevent society from knowing that zombies are real. Write about this task force. What does it take to keep the world blind from the truth? Does this task force ever make a mistake that causes society to find out?

204. A new energy source is discovered deep within the core of the earth. All countries ban the use and harvesting of this energy. Government explanations as to why are vague. Eventually, one country is pressured into harvesting this energy due to massive protests. Write about the nightmares found deep within the core of the Earth. What is the true reason for the ban of harvesting this energy?

205. Don't look outside. Don't peak around the curtain. You shouldn't even be in a room with a window. If you see the terror that is outside, it will notice you and kill you. Board all of your windows if you can. If you hear someone knock, don't answer.

206. It's not easy being a geek in school. Girls often overlook a guy like me. In this day and age, your zombie kill count is what impresses the ladies. The jocks have no problem keeping a high count with their baseball bats, hockey sticks, and lacrosse sticks. I've had it with having the lowest zombie kill count in school. Time to use my programming and science knowledge to my advantage.

207. A patient from an asylum for the most mentally disturbed individuals has a crush on one of the employees. At first, it seems innocent, but as months pass the employee finds the patient stalking her in different parts of the building. She finally transfers to a different position so that she doesn't have to encounter this patient any longer but begins to find small dandelions where ever she goes. She learns the patient has been picking them every day.

One night, she discovers a glass of water with dandelions on her kitchen counter. When she enters her bathroom, there are more. A trail of dandelions goes down the hallway pointing to her bedroom. What happens next?

208. I thought I had escaped the man with the chainsaw. As I stopped to catch my breath, I heard the sounds once more. Running was my only option. Yet the further I ran, the more chainsaws I heard.

209. Despite witnessing her boyfriend turn into a zombie, she was still receiving text messages from him. His phone was still in his pocket. How was this happening?

210. There's something beautiful about the sounds of the undead which was why I incorporated their moans into my music. I was asked to perform my music live with the undead at my performance. That's when everything went wrong.

211. A reality tv show presents a black rose to the cast member that is the next to die. All the contestants know they are sick with a terminal illness but participate in the show for money for their families.

In the latest episode, you are one of the audience members. The black rose presentation begins. You run through your mind guessing who you think will die next. The host of the show walks into the audience and hands you the black rose. This has never happened before. Why were you given the rose? Did you know of any terminal illness prior to the show?

212. The forest is thick with trees from young to old. During the day the forest is quiet. But at night it is as if all the trees are humming as a chorus. Little do the people who visit the forest know, a witch is trapping the souls of hikers and campers within the trees as a way to keep her forest lush and humming. Write about the witch. Is she ever discovered?

213. Scientists discover a way to make use of all the undead that have overpopulated the world. If certain sections of the brain are still intact, memories, knowledge, and data can be extracted. What kind of data is extracted? What is done with it? Does anyone object to what the scientists are doing?

214. "You may have known me as Nurse Melinda before…but today, for you, I am Lady Death. Your time has come."

215. While doing laundry in your basement, you notice another trap door under a rug leading even further down. Not remembering that door when buying your home, you become curious and head down below. You find piles of bones, organ jars, and a photography darkroom in the corner filled with torture victim photos. As you are about to race upstairs, your spouse stops you at the top of the steps.
"Finally, you found my lair. I knew someday you'd find this place. Now we are at a crossroads. Join me, or them."

216. What would a zombie invasion drill be like in schools? Write about the event that caused these drills to be practiced.

217. A new neighbor on the block stares out of their window at all hours of the day. Annoyed, the owner of the house across the street decides to find out why the neighbor keeps staring at their house.

The neighbor replies, "I'm watching over you. You may think you live alone, but you don't."

218. Write a slasher horror western with cowboys, gunslingers, saloons, and horses. Who are the victims? How do the townspeople try to protect themselves? Do they band together or work alone? Is there a hero among them?

219. A new zombie theme park comes to town. Every roller coaster has zombies thrashing on the sidelines. All of the food is zombie themed. Funhouses and mazes have real zombies in cages just far enough away to miss the park guests. Write about the day everything goes wrong.

220. Fisherman and jet skiers filled the lake that summer afternoon. Everything seemed like a typical day until the lake water began to boil. The most frightening part wasn't the blood-soaked lake or the screams. It was the dark shadows that covered the land on the edge of the water. There was nowhere to go except into the haunted fog.

221. This company promises to keep memories safe in case of sudden amnesia or dementia. A woman is suffering from memory loss and goes to her digital storage to retrieve them. But when she plugs her mind into the memory bank, something goes terribly wrong.

All of her memories still exist but disturbingly warped. However, she doesn't know the difference between the damaged memories and reality.

How does believing these memories are true psychologically affecting her?

222. "We need that demon spirit that you extracted...now."

"We have a problem...hopefully just a small problem."

"And what is that?"

"I put the spirt inside my nephew's bear in a panic when my home was raided."

"Okay, well then go get it."

"The problem is, my nephew got a plane early this morning before I woke up. I thought they weren't leaving until tomorrow."

"So you're telling me, a demon is on a plane with all those people right now?"

"They're heading to London as we speak."

223. An offbeat graveyard wedding is interrupted by a horde of zombies. At first, the bride thinks her wedding is ruined. But the groomsmen step in and take advantage of the situation in a creative way. How does the celebration continue? What did they do with the zombies?

224. Turning into a zombie isn't a quick process. It is often slow and undetected for weeks. Symptoms are similar to the flu and often misdiagnosed. Write about a group that sets out to kill anyone that shows even the slightest symptom of turning. Does anyone try to stop them?

225. You are watching a 3D horror movie with a couple of friends. Part way through the movie, images from the film appear warped and are pulling away from the screen. At first, you are annoyed by the movie images distorting. You then quickly realize that the frightening creatures that have pulled themselves from the screen as no longer part of the movie...but are actually inside the theater with you. Write what happens next.

226. The police station evidence room came to life: objects are rearranged, noises are heard on the other side of the wall, and items are damaged. When the security cameras are investigated, the footage goes fuzzy anytime something appears to start moving. A police officer volunteers to stay in the room for the night to see what is happening. What does he discover?

227. This art center accepts a new exhibit from a local artist every couple of weeks. The latest exhibit catches the eyes of horror fanatics. The frightening paintings are displayed the week of Halloween. But on the last night of the exhibit, all of the paintings come to life and attack the visitors.

228. The most popular reality show on television features an arena between the living and the undead. Though grotesque and deadly, it stays on the air because it has the highest television rating ever seen. What happens on this show?

229. Investigators and authorities had a hunch as to who was responsible for the missing bodies that showed up downstream. They called him River Man. But the man who worshiped his river god was not to be crossed. Write about a man who worships and makes human sacrifices to a river god. Who dares to investigate him?

230. Write about a quiet librarian that is building up a collection of books about witchcraft and dark magic in the basement of the public library. Does anyone ever notice her collection growing? What happens when she tries to conduct witchcraft in the library?

231. Write about a werewolf that hates his human side. He gnaws on his own bare flesh, talks as little as possible, and sleeps on the floor. He decides to seek out a sorcerer known for his dark arts and transformation. But something goes wrong with the ritual, leaving him permanently in-between states. Now stuck in a hideous disfigurement as half man half wolf, his resentment sends him into a rage to kill anyone who ever sets eyes on him. Why does he hate his human side so much?

232. Write a story about someone meeting their in-laws for the first time at a family BBQ. What happens when they notice their in-laws are cooking human brains on the grill right next to the hot dogs? How do they react?

233. Write about a famous author that somehow can defeat the zombie apocalypse with just his words. What does he write? How do his words matter?

234. A politician with a known coulrophobia (fear of clowns) is staying in a 4-star hotel for the week. A group of people that dislike him decide to organize a clown meetup, gathering as many people in clown costumes to stay at the hotel as well. With cameras following this politician he tries his best to play it cool, but eventually cannot control his anxiety. What was first supposed to be a joke, quickly spirals out of control. The politician is now trapped in the hotel with his wife and a few members of the media. The clowns are out for blood, empowered by their masks, numbers, and hatred. Write about his attempts to flee the locked down hotel where he is cut off from outside communication.

235. You are visiting a friend's gravestone that died in a war. Suddenly, all of the inscriptions disappear. No names. No dates. In the far corner of the graveyard, you notice one stone light up. Your name is on it.

You hear a voice say, "You must return all the names back to each gravestone. In order to do that, you must experience each death of the fallen yourself. Otherwise, this last stone will stay here with your name on it…and you will die."

Write about the experience.

236. Write about a character that must choose between joining a lifelong cult in college or forever be cursed and tormented by its members. What does this cult do? What happens to the people who refuse to join? How did this student get involved with them in the first place?

237. One year ago, I was bitten by a zombie. I acquired three years' worth of the vaccine in which I administer daily to prevent turning. Bandits stole half of my stash which left me just over a year left of the vaccine. Either I find a cure in the next year, or I turn.

238. Write a psychological horror about a woman that will go to any lengths to be noticed by her ex. She appears on tv shows he watches, radio ads, and billboards. Though she is not contacting him directly, he knows she is doing this to torment him. Where does he draw the line? How can he escape it?

239. You wake up strapped down to a chair. Each hand is holding onto a remote that controls a drip IV.
"Welcome," a voice begins over the intercom. "You have been given a choice today. You can choose between one of the two IVs attached to you. Choose the left, and you will face pain. Choose the right, and you will face all your fears. Decide now or both IVs will start."

240. A group of space pioneers crash land on a distant planet. The scanners conclude that the land is habitable. There is vegetation, air, and the right amount of gravity. After spending several days on the planet, they notice the weather getting increasingly dangerous. They take shelter in their ship and research more about the planet they are on.

They discover they are on a haunted planet, abandoned by all forms of intelligent life. Only plants and insects remain.

The planet makes every effort to kill and terrify anyone who dares to stay too long.

Write about their struggle to survive this haunted planet while the crew fixes their ship.

241. A police recruit in training is on a route with a veteran officer. In between the dispatcher's calls, a mysterious voice cuts in and out. The recruit wants to investigate, but the veteran officer tells him, "You don't want to get involved with these messages – it's safer this way."

The voice disappears and is replaced by screams.

The recruit is horrified and questions further but is told to never speak of it again.

After being officially sworn in as a police officer, he decides to investigate the strange reoccurring messages for himself.

242. Write about an asylum patient that can pull the minds of nearby people into his nightmare thoughts. How do the workers protect themselves from his powers? What kind of images does he place in people's minds? What happens when all precautions no longer work?

243. The plane you are on is losing altitude fast. Miraculously, the pilot gains enough control to keep the plane in the air. Suddenly, you notice the passengers one by one turning into the undead. How do you survive?

244. Write about a digital marketer that notices something suspicious about an internet trend. The spike in specific keyword searches and social media accounts lead the marketer to believe either a cult is arising right under everyone's nose or it is code for some kind of human trafficking ring. To what lengths of research does this marketer go to find the truth? Do they ever contact authorities or try to uncover everything themselves?

245. During surgery, a patient's heart stops. His chest is completely cut open. Doctors and nurses make every effort to bring him back to life. Just as they are about to call the time of death, the man's eyes open. Even though he is still cut open and his heart has stopped, he is wide awake. And he is not happy.

246. Write about a journal that writes days of entries at a time on its own. This journal finds itself in the hands of different people throughout history. A horrifying fate comes true for each and every person that possesses the journal. What does it say? How do the entries appear?

247. A man is infected with the zombie virus but discovers a way to stop it from progressing any further. The virus has given him a few new skills without killing him. However, he is hindered by the upkeep of his discovered remedy. What does he have to do to keep himself from completely turning? What special abilities has he acquired from the virus?

248. Write about a parallel world to ours where every human on Earth is a zombie. Unfortunately, this parallel world is starting to overlap and seep into our world absent of zombies. Do people ever encounter their zombie self? Why are the worlds colliding?

249. A tomb is discovered almost 20 feet below the ground. Archeologists are convinced they know who it belongs to and eagerly open it up. At the edge of the tomb is a beautiful sarcophagus carved in gold. But before they have a chance to investigate further, undead soldiers awaken and approach the archeologists. They are surrounded, fearing for their lives.

SECTION 6: PROMPTS 250 - 300

250. After winning a writer's grant, an author moves to a secluded town for six months to write his novel. After a month of strange occurrences, he begins to question if the town is being manipulated by a witch that wishes to harvest the souls of the innocent. Unsure by his speculation, the author investigates and researches deeper. He soon finds himself the witch's next target.

251. A man with the ability to jump into people's minds is hired by a team of investigators to solve a mysterious murder that occurred in a historic mansion. The more he unravels from his mind hopping, the more frightened he becomes. He begins to question if demons from hell had a hand in the unexplained murder.

252. Write about protestors that are against the extermination of zombies. Why do they want to keep them around? How do they fight for their cause?

253. "No, I can't leave you."

"You must...leave me behind and save yourself."

"No, I literally can't leave you. My flesh is fusing with yours."

254. What if memories could be swapped back and forth between people? Imagine a world where if you lived a horrible event, you could pass it on to a person of your choosing to relive it in their mind instead. Are there any restrictions? Imagine a society where bad memories could be passed on to specific people as punishment for crimes. What kind of memories are passed on? What happens when someone receives one?

255. The zombie apocalypse breaks out while you are at the fairgrounds. You just completed a hot dog competition and have a major stomach ache as a result. Are you able to outrun the zombies and survive? Write about what happens next.

256. Expert hunters are hired to capture any monster people claim to be a myth such as the Loch Ness Monster, Big Foot, or a Chupacabra. Write about their hunt and how it all goes terribly wrong just as they believe to have captured something out of legends.

257. Write about an underground organization where people bet and compete in zombie fighting. Where do the zombies come from? How is a winner determined? Do zombies fight each other or living humans?

258. Unloaders at a big box retail store receive an unmarked package. Out of laziness, employees ignore the box. Days later, one employee decides to take care of it. He expects toys to be inside because of the occasional rattling. Instead, he discovers the box to be empty. Ever since opening the box, the store feels haunted. The aura is off and strange occurrences happen at least once a week. Write about the haunted store.

259. A new company arrives in the center of the city focusing on helping people get a good night sleep. Because you have been having the same reoccurring dream of the end of the world, you set up an appointment. The service they offer allows you to jump into other people's dreams instead of your own. You sign a waiver, understanding that not all dreams are positive. There are no promises as to what kind of dream you'll experience. After sleeping there for one night, you are troubled by your recent dreams. Someone else has had very similar dreams as you. Why is this happening? Are you able to find who is having the same dream as you? Are the dreams prophesizing what is to come?

260. Write about a doctor that secretly conducts experiments on hospital patients in order to make zombies a reality. How does he continue his research without being discovered?

261. The last bus for the night never comes. You wait on the bench for it, despite how late it is because it is your only way home. Finally, over an hour later the bus shows up. You enter and find your usual seat. It isn't until after you look up from your book that you notice your regular driver isn't there. A skeleton man is driving the bus. All other riders are skeletons too.

262. A natural disaster hits a small town, causing dozens of families to flee to a church at the edge of town for safety. Though the church is still open to weekly worship, very few people are ever seen entering. As time passes, people are noticing that something is off about the priest. Becoming unsettled, some decide to brave the storms instead of sticking around. It is then that all the doors are suddenly locked from the outside. What happens next?

263. A rumor at a local technical college has been circulating for years that there is always at least one person out of woodworking class that loses a finger. While taking the class for yourself, you unexpectedly discover the truth. Not only are the rumors true, you are to be the next victim. Why are students losing their fingers in this woodworking class? Why has no one ever come forward with the truth before?

264. The new surgeon hired at the hospital was said to be the best. But when the staff and hospital director are unable to brainwash him into following their horrified practices of harvesting organs and draining blood from unsuspecting patients, he must fight to not only save the lives of the patients but also himself. Why must he stay with this hospital? How does he fight to survive the corrupt practices?

265. Hundreds of people gather at the beach one sunny afternoon. As everyone is enjoying their day, a giant sea creature washes ashore - dead. No official can immediately identify what it is. Years later, scientists conclude where the dangerous creature came from and locate more of its kind. What kind of danger does this newly identified sea creature pose? How did no one notice it before?

266. This adult-only corn maze is the most popular Halloween attraction in the surrounding area. There are food trucks and places to purchase alcoholic beverages. But a terrifying event turns the maze into mass panic and chaos. What happens within the maze? What is causing people to run, screaming in terror?

267. A charity organization opens, promising to cure the infected across the world. For just $20 a month, subscribers can help cure up to five zombies a year by providing a lifesaving antidote, housing, and transportation back home. Write about this organization and if people are truly being saved by it. How did people become zombies in the first place? How is this charity advertised? Could there be a dark truth behind this charity?

268. This inmate was kept in solitary confinement six days a week for the last 30 years. The one day a week he is allowed to mingle with other prisoners, he never speaks or interacts in any way. Most inmates and security guards aren't even sure what his initial crime was. The original staff from 30 years prior had long retired.
One day, the inmate snaps. He fights his way through security and escapes jail. Prison staff digs up his old records to discover his history. His haunting past shakes everyone to their core. Who is he? What were his past crimes?

269. Write about a shapeshifting serial killer that can change into almost anyone. How does he choose his victims? What are his limits in shapeshifting? Is he ever caught?

270. Before the gastropub closes for the night, a horde of zombies fills the streets outside. Only six people are left in the bar. Two of them are too drunk to take care of themselves. Two of the customers are only buzzed and are soon to sober up. The other two are staff members: the bartender and the manager. Write about these six people and how they plan to handle the apocalypse. Do they plan to escape or hide and wait it out?

271. Rumor has it, that anyone who ventures through this forest will eventually commit suicide within the next year. Many stories confirm these claims, but many are still skeptics. Write about a group of filmmakers creating a documentary about this forest. To gather more data, a handful of volunteers agree to go through this forest to prove the claims are false. What happens during the filming?

272. The power throughout town is out. Fixing powerlines won't bring the power back as it is sourced to be a few switches turned off at the electric plant. However, everyone that enters the building to turn the switches back on goes missing. With the power now out for days and no sign of life in the power plant, a team goes in to see what has happened to everyone. Why are people disappearing?

273. A family under witness protection is sent to a beach house to live in. But every time the tide rises, a dark spirit can be seen at the edge of the water. The family is frightened by the sight but continues to live out their days. Each week the tide gets a little stronger, creeping closer to the beach house. Write about what happens when the ghost gets too close to the house.

274. Write about a survivor of an exorcism and their psychological trauma since then. What do they remember from the exorcism? What events trigger their trauma? Does their experience change how they view the world?

275. Write a psychological thriller about a young couple getting lost on a road trip and ending up in a small town that doesn't exist on the map. No matter how many times their mind brings them back to reality, telling them to leave, they somehow keep returning to a foggy state of confusion. The town is twisted and frightening, yet they cannot clear their minds enough to leave. What happens?

276. Choose a major war in history and add zombies as one of the opposing sides. Who would use a zombie army to their advantage? Were the zombies once soldiers? Or did the army trap people who were already zombies?

277. After a near death experience, she is stuck with irreparable brain damage and paralysis. As she recovers, she notices that she can see things she never has before. Dark figures shifting across the room or a glimpse into the future, are just a few of the things she can see. Eventually, she embraces her gift. But this makes the dark spirits of the night want to come for her soul all the more.

278. The witch could pacify any zombie's craving with her creamy soup, blended with herbs and spices. But the same soup that calms a zombie is what turned them in the first place. Write about how this witch lures unsuspecting victims to eat her poisoned soup.

279. A little bit of science and a dash of witchcraft in 8th-grade science class creates a lifeform impossible to control. But after facing the teacher about it, they quickly realize that was their first mistake. What was the teacher's reaction? What kind of creature did they create?

280. A time traveler comes to warn people of the impending zombie apocalypse. But every time he tries to warn someone, they do not believe him. Tell a story of a time traveler that journeys to different moments in time in search of the right person to believe him. How do they defeat the zombies together?

281. Write about voice-controlled devices in homes that have established a dark, murderous AI of its own. What other appliances does it control? How does it torment homeowners? Is there any way to shut it off? What does the machine want to accomplish?

282. It is your great-grandmother's 105th birthday party. Right before she is about to blow out the candles, you notice her flesh dripping off her bones. At first, you think this is due to old age. Luckily, you realize right before being bitten that she is transforming into a zombie. Not all of your relatives are so lucky. Write about what happens next.

283. As the hostage situation appears to intensify, a veteran police officer makes his way in to negotiate. Camera crews surround the area as people worry about their loved ones. But what people don't realize right away is the police officer is working with the captors. Write about the hostage situation and the events that unfold in the point-of-view of the hostages.

284. A murder mystery event in an old wine cellar takes a tragic turn. No one can escape. And no help is coming.

285. The last war survivor is turning 100 and having a birthday party in celebration. After the party, he pulls his great-grandson aside and tells him of a secret that has never been revealed before about the war.

"I taped my diary under the mattress. Read it. I am the last person alive that was there. They can't do anything to me now." That night, the man dies. The next afternoon the great-grandson retrieves the diary, revealing a dark secret. The world is in danger. What does he discover?

286. Zombies cannot survive on land. Instead, tens of thousands are multiplying within all bodies of water. Because there is more water on the planet than land, this type of outbreak is devastating and impossible to defeat. Write about the zombies that live in the water.

287. This small decorative item is haunted and making its way from one estate sale to the next. It seems anyone who keeps this piece of decor ends up dying not long after. Write about the last person to bring this item home from a sale and the series of events that unfold before their life is in danger. Can they survive its curse?

288. A beloved band is killed in a tragic accident when their van launches off a bridge over the river. Since the accident, the bar that was planned to be their next gig has become haunted by the dead band members. Write about this haunting. Are the spirits friendly or frightening? Who notices the spirits? Does the bar thrive or lose business over it?

289. An illustrated book is found to frighten children on the same page every time. Adults can't figure out why since the pictures and story are uplifting and fun. What is scaring the children? How did the parents come together and discover this mutual problem? Social media? Web forum? Parent groups?

290. To become the next chief, one must cross through the haunted forest. But when the future chief enters this forest, he discovers that there is nothing haunted about it. There are no spirits or ghosts to be seen. Instead, there is a dangerous beast lurking. This beast is being controlled by a tribe of hungry cannibals. Write about his attempts to survive. Does he make it back to his people to tell them the truth?

291. A series of murders has peaked the interest of an out of town detective. No matter how much evidence he looks at, the trail goes cold. That is until his 5th week investigating when he notices a troubling correlation between the murders and a local newspaper comic strip. How are they connected? What kind of murder clues are found within the comic?

292. This small section of the United States has segregated from the rest of the country. However, it is not marked anywhere in maps or history books.

Write about one person or a group that gets lost and stumbles upon this area. Not only do they face horrors from within, but also cannot escape it. The United States government has no authority over the area and cannot save them. Who lives there? What kind of torments do they face?

293. Write about five best friends in middle school that team up to defeat a single zombie discovered in their teacher's basement. How do they prepare for the battle? Why does their teacher have a zombie trapped in the wall of his basement?

294. Write about a serial killer that sews animal parts on his victims and puts them on display for the town to see. Sometimes it's just a deer leg instead of an arm, a boar's head, or half an elk's body. The town is afraid – but can't seem to find someone to crack the case.

295. A car without its lights on is following you in the dark. Afraid, you call the police and tell them about the person behind you. The police arrive and ultimately pull you over instead. The car without its lights pulls over behind the police. The person driving the car emerges along with the police officer. They appear to be working together. What happens next?

296. Zombies were officially defeated 50 years ago. Write about a team of filmmakers that are putting together a documentary about the apocalypse. Who do they interview for the film? What secrets do they uncover?

297. Zombies invade a comic book convention. Write about a group of geeks combating a horde of zombies in their cosplay outfits. Are any of their prop weapons strong enough to defeat zombies with?

298. He remembers all too well the years of his father as an exorcist. The sounds. The words. The smell. It's been 15 years since he has witnessed an exorcism. He is grown up with a family. His father is dead. And for the most part, he rarely thinks about the exorcisms. That is until the demons of the past seem to have found him. They want revenge. And the only one left is him. Write a story about the man facing past demons that want payback.

299. Captured zombies run in the same direction on an oversized spinning hamster wheel to form the latest environmentally friendly energy source. These underground wheels keep the lights on above the surface. Write about a dystopian society that is just beginning to learn the truth about the zombie hordes underground. Do the zombies live forever, or do new people have to be infected to keep the power on?

300. The zombie virus has been in you for years. You have been able to control it through regular feedings of brains. Only one of your friends knows you are infected as you lead a relatively normal life. You decide to compete in a cooking contest that consists of incorporating surprise ingredients into a creative dish. In the final round, you are up against one other. The final ingredient: brains. Do you maintain your composure? What happens next?

ABOUT THE AUTHOR

Julie Wenzel grew up in a small town in central Minnesota. After graduating with a bachelor's degree in mass communications, she turned her focus to creative writing.

Besides writing, Julie enjoys art and video games in her spare time. She currently resides in the suburbs of Minneapolis, Minnesota.

Made in the USA
Monee, IL
04 February 2021